MAD Money:

12 Foundational Principles To Make
More Money In Half The Time With
Half The Stress

JOE A SIMMONS

JOE A SIMMONS

ISBN-13: 978-1-63227-275-1

TABLE OF CONTENTS

PROLOGUE

Dear Reader,

Money is a confrontational subject to talk about. We have different conflicting perspectives about it. This book is intended to inform you about how money works and the foundational principles to attract more money in your career and life. This book is a beginner's guide and is not intended to provide everything there is to know about money. I was motivated to write this book because so many people are struggling when it comes to making more money. A common question I get "How do I make more money?" I hope this book adds value to you. You have decided to dedicate your precious time to read it. My wish for you is to learn from this book, so that you can apply the principles and achieve your desired financial status.

Let's begin!

See you inside.

Best Wishes,

Joe A. Simmons

PART I – MASTERY

This is a very interesting question I get asked all the time.

More than 50% of Americans are living paycheck-to-paycheck and are so close to experiencing financial stress and turmoil.

The answer to this question is simple but hard to achieve for most.

If you have not already guessed the answer or looked at the top of the page the answer is *mastery*.

MASTERY IS THE ANSWER

Mastery is the ultimate and fastest way to attract money to you and your career.

I know this may come as a shocking surprise.

No one has told you that mastery is the answer to this money question.

I thought about the answer to this question long and hard.

The number one commonality all successful people share is mastery.

HIGH INCOME EARNERS

High income earners have obtained financial information that majority of the population does not have.

High income earners control over 90% of all the money that is made in the trillion dollar global marketplace.

High income earners engage in activities and daily habits that allow them to attract large quantities of money with ease.

WORK ON YOUR CRAFT

The real secret to mastery is internal instead of external as the majority believe.

Majority of the population believes the answer to attracting money is external because they make the fatal mistake of chasing money.

Chasing money leads to unnecessary frustration, stress, and wasted valuable time.

We cannot get valuable time back.

Do not chase the latest trend or hack.

7 Financial Trends to Achieve Your Financial Dreams in 2018.

10 Financial Hacks for 2019.

These headline titles are misleading.

Be careful engaging and reading these headlines.

Work on your craft.

Be the best that you can be.

Be the best at what you do in your industry.

Why don't more people work on their craft?

Work is required to improve in your craft.

Most people are not willing to commit.

Some of us want the easy answer and immediate results.

"Every good thing will not come easy, you have to be willing to work for what you want to experience in life."

LEVELS OF MASTERY

Working on your craft will allow you to achieve different levels of mastery.

Yes, there are levels to mastery.

You must complete them one level at a time.

Most people only achieve the first two levels which is a tragedy.

I believe people have so much undeveloped potential that can produce massive career results and happiness.

5 LEVELS OF MASTERY

The five levels of mastery are Novice, Amateur, Professional, Master, and Legend.

NOVICE

A novice is just beginning their career.

A novice may also choose to stay at this level because the least amount of dedication, commitment, and sacrifice is required.

This level is dangerous because there is very little growth.

Novice experiences the highest levels of frustration.

AMATEUR

The novice develops and becomes an amateur.

An amateur is average in talent, time, and skill.

An amateur completes the basic requirements for their current position.

An amateur becomes easily distracted.

Amateurs enjoy more recreation time than career balance.

An amateur is happy confessing that he or she is average.

Amateurs do not place high standards on themselves to achieve progress in their life and career.

PROFESSIONAL

Majority of the population likes to believe they are professionals.

This is a huge delusion.

Professionals study, strategize, and execute.

Professionals are extremely focused on their goals and are not easily distracted.

Professionals understand that adversity and challenges are ahead.

The reasons for obtaining their goals are more important than letting a current challenge stop them.

Professional create high standards for themselves and are their worst critics.

MASTER

After years and countless hours of dedication you can achieve the level of master.

Obtaining this level is extremely difficult.

At the master level we will experience high levels of success and low levels of struggle and adversity.

The master invest heavily in personal and professional development.

The master is conscious of his or her environment.

The master seeks out the best mentors and coaches.

The master is disciplined and carefully selects the individuals they choose to let in their professional and social circles.

LEGEND

We all have heard legendary stories about people who have achieved great success.

Legendary people are willing to make extremely difficult decisions.

Individuals on lower levels will have negative opinions about you when you reach the legend status.

As a legend remain confident in your skills and abilities.

You can handle negativity expressed toward you.

Legends invest massive amounts about of time in to their crafts' affecting other areas of their life.

Legends have developed extreme love affairs with their crafts.

This love affair is the "real oxygen" in legends' lives.

They are no longer pursing financial rewards.

 The opportunity to continue doing what they love is the ultimate career joy and happiness.

TALENT, TIME, AND SKILLS

Talent, Time, and Skills.

Talent is DNA given to us by our parents.

We can't control our talent.

I recommend we find a career field that allows our talent to develop.

We become extremely passionate about a career field that doesn't allow for our talent to reach its highest potential.

This is a huge mistake.

A common career mistake is comparing ourselves to others and wishing we had their talents.

Celebrate your talent and develop your skills.

Time and Skills are two things you can control.

How much time do you want to devote to mastery?

"We make time for things that are extremely important to us at the current moment."

FOUNDATIONAL PRINCIPLES TO MASTERY

There are four foundational principles when practiced consistently will increase your mastery proficiency.

Knowledge, Continual Learning, Practice, and Adaptability are the "magic four".

Knowledge: We should learn the basics of our career industry and all that we can to become the person we were meant to be.

Continual Learning: We should strive to always learn something new.

Practice: This should be a must but is optional for most.

Practice is an opportunity for improvement and growth.

Adaptability: This foundational principle is difficult for most people to execute as life is constantly changing especially in your career.

I recommend you change as well.

Your health will thank you for it.

PRINCIPLE 1:
KNOWLEDGE

KNOWLEDGE SHOULD BE A FIRST PRIORITY

First things first.

When we are attempting to attract money we need to focus on gaining knowledge.

Knowledge is needed when you start your career or transition into a new one.

Knowledge is similar to learning a language.

Master the language so that you can communicate with others.

As a collective population we overlook or skip this crucial step.

We wonder why we are not achieving the results we seek.

Seek knowledge and understanding.

They will lead us to less mistakes, accelerated growth and achievement.

OBSESSIONAL LOVE AFFAIR

Pursuing a career you love is very important.

I personally believe that our career choices should be similar to a romantic relationship with a potential or current love interest.

Initially we have interest.

We move on to passion.

Passion can potentially be a good obsession.

Successful people and high income earners are obsessed with their industries and careers.

They could not imagine doing anything else.

They are obsessed.

They would miss their career so much that health consequences could arise.

KNOWLEDGE COMES WITH TIME

"Knowledge comes with time."

This is a hard concept for most of us to swallow.

We can become knowledgeable in any career we chose.

We have to give it time.

Becoming knowledgeable will not happen overnight.

Be patient.

Remaining patient when developing knowledge is easier to say than to actually do.

When you rush you are limiting your development and growth.

"Every expert started as a beginner and became the expert you know today."

A common mistake we make is comparing our beginning knowledge to an expert's current knowledge resource bank.

This is completely unfair to us.

KNOWLEDGABLE EXPRESSION

Understanding intellectual concepts is great.

True knowledge is expressed through action.

Good intentions is not enough.

Knowledgeable expression is proof.

We know what we say we know.

The good news for us is that we do not have to be knowledgeable with our first experiences.

When you don't know or understand something just admit it.

We can make a decision to know more or not about the topic.

KNOWLEDGE REQUIRES PATIENCE

Knowledge is not developed or obtained immediately.

Unfortunately, some of us believe so.

This is why we do not develop the knowledge we seek and need.

When we start anything new it usually takes time.

When we were infants' it took time to learn how to walk.

Our parents had to have patience that we would walk in time.

"Knowledge can't be developed or obtained without patience.
Be patient and all the knowledge you desire has the potential to
be yours. "

We like to be very subjective when applying patience in certain areas
of our lives.

REMAIN CALM: THERE WILL BE MISTAKES AND FAILURES

I completely understand wanting to do the best you can in everything
that you attempt.

There will mistakes and failures.

This is where the most valuable learning lessons are.

Remember mistakes and failures will be a part of the process.

You have the opportunity to discover those hidden gems of
knowledge.

Do not get upset when mistakes and failures happen.

Everything will work out.

Continue forward.

"Failures provide wisdom and guidance to assist on the success journey."

Every successful person has failed at something in their career.

Successful people agree with this statement.

I can personally attest.

I have obtained some of my greatest career knowledge from my mistakes and failures.

I am currently a corporate trainer, results coach, and consultant at a financial service company.

My colleagues consider me to be a knowledgeable resource.

I am honored and flattered that my colleagues think that highly of me.

The truth is that I have made almost every mistake they have made and more.

I also have failed a lot.

My failures have rewarded me with current knowledge.

My colleagues have a hard time believing that I have failed and made mistakes.

The reason they don't believe me is because my failures and mistakes were conducted in private.

In addition some of them were not employed with the company when these failures and mistakes occurred.

KNOWLEDGE EXPLORATION & DISCOVERY

I want to challenge you to view obtaining knowledge as an exploration and discovery.

When we start an exploration our excitement and curiosity are at peak levels.

As we continue the exploration, we wonder how this journey is going to turn out.

What surprises lie ahead.

Discovery is about having determination to find what you seek.

Exploration like discovery should be pleasurable.

(Note: Exploration is going deep in knowledge, Discovery is going far in knowledge)

COMMON ACTION: KNOWLEDGE

It pains me to write this.

I personally believe so many of us are hurting ourselves when it comes to achieving our career goals.

The common action we take is gaining adequate or basic knowledge.

We think this will be sufficient for the remainder of our career.

I honestly believe that most of us know and understand that this is not true.

However, we commit this common action when it comes to knowledge.

RECOMMENDED ACTION: KNOWLEDGE

The solution is to learn as much as you can.

When you learn as much as you can your career opportunities become endless.

I whole heartily believe this to be true.

Wanting immediate and high returns on our time for learning something new is why we do not learn as much as possible.

You will be rewarded for the knowledge that you obtained but it will not be immediate.

Do not steal from your future because you are focused on your present wants.

PRINCIPLE 2: CONTINUAL LEARNING

Everyone knows that you should learn something more than once.

Unfortunately, we learn then stop.

We do this in our careers constantly.

I highly recommend that we invest in continual learning.

Our future selves will thank us.

Continual learning is optional.

We engage in continual learning casually becoming career casualties.

CONSTANLY CHANGING BUT NOT YOU?

Your career industry is constantly changing.

Don't you want to change with it?

I understand that change and continual learning is not an entertaining process.

24

We neglect continual learning and increase the odds of getting left behind in our careers.

Getting left behind in our careers becomes an unpleasant experience.

I recommend that when our industries' change, we learn about the changes.

Create new strategies and execute accordingly to the changes.

New strategies lead to new rewards.

A BEGINNER'S MIND

Continual learning has taught me the valuable lesson of having a beginner's mind.

We all want to be experts in life including our careers.

This mindset puts a lot of stress on the brain.

The pre-frontal cortex attempts to cypher all the bits of information.

I give you permission to have a beginner's mind.

Starting at the bottom leads to a lot of growth.

Maintaining a beginner's mind can sometimes lead to a huge breakthrough.

We do not help ourselves by trying to be experts when we are not.

All we do is delay ourselves from being exposed later in life.

When we are beginners' and admit what we do not know others are willing to help us if we ask.

CLOSED MINDED

I personally believe "being closed minded" is one of the quickest ways to create chaos and havoc in your career and life.

I believe closed mindedness is like a disease that spreads quickly throughout your body.

Unfortunately, closed mindedness is a strong decision.

This decision can be changed at any time we choose.

I have worked with several colleagues' in the past who were closed minded.

They became "victims" in their minds.

Psychologically they created this.

Closed mindedness yields entitlement and arrogance.

The results are a quick, hard, and painful career fall.

COMPETITVE ADVANTAGE

Continual learning is a high performer's competitive advantage.

High performers know that only 10-20% of their competitors are willing to invest in continual learning.

Investing in continual learning creates a huge advantage and separation from others.

I have used this competitive advantage and it is highly effective.

I understand you may not be as competitive as I am.

If you are a competitive person you will see amazing results when applied.

Everyone wants to be a winner.

Talk is cheap.

We must do.

Producing results express what you want.

STAYING AHEAD OF THE PACK

Continual learning allows you to stay ahead of the pack.

The worst place to be is at the end of the pack.

Most of us are there.

We stay there for most of our lives.

Staying ahead of the pack will help with your career branding, marketing, networking, and overall career.

You will create a strong brand.

Your brand will stand out from others.

Creating and or strengthening curiosity and attraction.

Your marketing will be unique and valuable.

People will want to network with you instead of you always having to chase them.

When you retire do you want to be remembered as someone who stayed ahead of the pack?

Or someone who remained at the end of the pack?

COMMON ACTION: CONTINUAL LEARNING

Is continual learning really worth it?

I don't think so.

This is a common thought that most of us will ask ourselves.

What is the immediate return on investment if I invest my time in continual learning?

How much money can I make in the next hour?

How much money can I make at the end of the day?

How much money can I make by the end of the week?

How much money can I make at the end of the month?

I now have to decide to make personal and career sacrifices to participate in continual learning.

I will pass.

RECOMMENDED ACTION: CONTINUAL LEARNING

I recommend developing and improving to be the best we can be.

Successful people and high income earners invest in continual learning.

We should want to join this exclusive group.

If we develop and maintain the same habits, activities, and strategies as successful people and high income earners we should get the same results they do.

I understand continual learning is not a short term investment and payoff.

If I commit to this new plan and execute daily I increase my chances of achieving my career goals.

I will shift my focus from money to improvement.

When we improve and grow money will be attracted to us.

Continual learning is similar to building a house.

The process is long term but yields amazing results.

PRINCIPLE 3: PRACTICE

Repetition is the key to everything in life.

Unfortunately, when it comes to our career, we are not willing to believe or execute this concept.

Sometimes I become frustrated with my colleagues and others I interact with when it comes to practice.

Practice is a principle that is 100% percent in your control.

I completely understand practicing in a task repeatedly is not the most glamourous.

Practice can produce results that are worthwhile.

High performers love repetition.

High performers engage in practice because it allows them to enhance their competitive advantage and skill proficiency in their career field.

LEARN TO LOVE PRACTICE

We should learn to love practice.

We learn to love other concepts and activities but why not practice.

If we love practice it will love us in return.

We have to initiate the process first.

Successful people will tell you that they practice every day.

Practice grants them the opportunities to achieve their career goals.

"Practice is important."

"Practice prepares you for game time situations."

"Consistent practice can increase your comfort zone and decrease nervousness and anxiety."

PRACTICE INCREASES.....

This next statement may be shocking.

Practice increases confidence and competence.

I want to repeat that one more time so that it registers in your brain.

Practice increase confidence and competence.

Notice I mentioned confidence first, before competence.

The main reason why confidence increases with practice is because of progress.

We develop reference and recall points engaging in the law of familiarity.

I know I just said a mouthful.

I will explain further so that can comprehend what I am saying.

When we practice, we make progress.

Progress can be immediate, short-term or long term.

Every time we practice and make progress, we are creating reference points.

Reference points informs our mind of past experiences regarding practicing a particular activity.

Reference points develop over time to become recall points.

Recall points are deep conscious thoughts.

Recall points allows us to flashback to previous experiences.

We visualize the outcome we seek.

Recall points increase your confidence as well.

We are reminded if we successfully completed a similar task, we can do it again.

The law of familiarity activates.

The Law of familiarity makes us feel safe, confident, and competent.

The current experience becomes repetition.

All we have to do is repeat the same action(s) we did previously and we will experience the same results.

HOW GREAT DO YOU WANT TO BE IN YOUR CAREER?

The answer to this question is based entirely on what is important to you in your career.

Your ambition level will determine your career goals and outcomes.

Do not compare yourself to others.

I wrote that statement as a reminder to myself.

I know that I am guilty of that.

Learn self-awareness.

Be happy with what you want in your career.

Don't feel bad about it.

I believe a lot of ambitious people suffer with self-awareness.

I have worked with several colleagues who love work life balance.

My colleagues have confessed they love working 9 am to 5 pm.

This makes them happy in their career.

They are completely self-aware and unapologetic about their decision.

I love the process of working and creating new things.

I could not just work 9 am to 5 pm that would drive me crazy.

I feel like I would be cheating myself and the world the opportunity to make mankind a better place.

I am self-aware and confident in my decision to achieve greatness in my own way.

Achieving greatness is not about how many hours you are working.

Greatness is about happiness and self-awareness.

We all have the potential to reach greatness.

Greatness has many levels.

To reach the highest levels of greatness you will have to push your limits.

See what you truly can accomplish.

Make the impact you seek in the world.

PRACTICE SCHEDULE

Scheduling your day in advance increases your productivity.

This is so true.

I strongly recommend making practice apart of our daily schedules.

The most successful athletes, entertainers, entrepreneurs, and high performers do it.

We can also do it.

We schedule personal activities to shop for groceries, attend musical events, take vacations or spending time with loved ones.

I encourage us to schedule practice for our careers.

When scheduling practice do not view it as a chore but as an opportunity to develop and grow.

THE GREAT DIVIDER

I do not like to mention this but practice separates people.

This great divider as I refer to it applies to every area of your life especially our careers.

I learned this concept early in my career.

I remember being the new person at the company.

I observed the habits of my seasoned colleagues.

They did not practice well.

I slowly started to practice more and more.

The separation gap between them and me started to decrease drastically.

This great divider is also a part of the reason why I passed on a managerial position in the past.

If I accepted the managerial position, I would not have the same opportunities to practice.

I personally feel I would not as valuable to my team and division as I could potentially be because of atrophy.

At the current writing and future publication of this book my senior management team believes in the concept of "extreme delegation".

Extreme Delegation is when an authority figure no longer practices and improves.

The authority figure's main job is just to delegate everything.

The team should do all the heavy lifting.

I personally believe the most important character trait of a leader or authority figure is resourcefulness.

How can we be resourceful when we are so far removed from the ground?

We ascend toward the clouds and lose comprehension of what is taking place on the ground.

OUTWARD EXPRESSION

Practice is an outward expression of commitment and dedication.

We all know that talk is cheap just like bubblegum.

However, everyday people make confessions and declarations that are not congruent with their actions.

In my humble opinion what you say and do should be symmetric.

In order to be successful and achieve career happiness your thoughts, words, and actions need to be in alignment.

If you want to have massive influence and impact in the world you should practice daily.

I remember people would tell me.

"I want to achieve the same results you have."

"I want to achieve excellence just like you have."

I encourage them to go for it.

Less than a week later they are back to their normal habits.

I watch what people do not what they say.

One of my ultimate career goals is to become a successful film producer.

Hollywood film industry has a common understanding.

"90% of people fail in the entertainment business because they talk about what they are going to do instead of doing what they want to.

PRACTICE VIEWS

Practice can be seen as an opportunity or an obstacle.

I would like to challenge you to look at the former.

Life is filled with opportunities.

We will only find these opportunities if we see them.

Most of us see obstacles and think why should we bother?

We have not engaged or committed to personal development.

Limited or lack of personal development makes professional development harder.

By nature, your brain is a survival mechanism.

The only responsibility it has is to keep you alive, avoid struggle and pain.

Practice will challenge you.

The process will not be easy but it can be worth it.

Another reason why practice is seen as an obstacle is because we are progress driven animals.

Practice delays the results that we seek.

Persistence and determination will be required to obtain the progress goal.

PRIVATE PRACTICE

"People who work hard in private are rewarded and respected in public."

"People who are casual in private are exposed in public."

If this is your first time hearing this just marinate on that statement for a minute.

We all admire certain individuals in society and think highly of them.

Most of us fail to realize that the practice that is being done in private produces the amazing public results and rewards.

Successful music artists' have intense practice sessions because they want to produce the best performance they can.

One of the most successful entrepreneurs of all time would practice his presentation for days.

He wanted to ensure that when it was time to deliver his presentation he was ready.

His audiences enjoy and remember those iconic presentations.

We do not have to be one of the most successful of all time…. to achieve high levels of public rewards.

MUSCLE MEMORY & INSTINCTS

Practice assist in the growth of muscle memory and instincts.

We are creatures of habit.

The more practice we complete the more we condition our minds to be accustom to certain situations in life.

Reference and recall points transcend to the second level which is muscle memory.

Our default paradigm changes and muscle memory replace it.

Paradigms are thought patterns or certain beliefs held about what is achievable and unachievable.

As previously mentioned, your brain is a survival mechanism wanting to prevent tension from occurring in your life.

The ultimate level of practice is instincts.

At the instincts level very little thought is consulted.

You just do.

Your mind and body know what actions you need to execute in the present moment to achieve a goal or resolve a problem.

Do not suppress your instincts, develop and trust them.

COMMON ACTION: PRACTICE

We practice with no enthusiasm and passion.

This is a huge mistake.

We do not fully understand this magical gift we are given.

We take it for granted.

Then it is too late.

I have seen colleagues who did or stop practicing with passion and enthusiasm and their results started to decline leading to their termination at the company.

These colleagues became angry toward the company.

They played the role of victim.

They created career chaos for themselves.

RECOMMENDED ACTION: PRACTICE

The main reason for practice is preparation.

Preparation increases confidence and competence.

Make the decision to dedicate time to practice.

Practice gives you a preview of what is to come.

When we are prepared, there will be little to no surprises.

When challenges arise you will already have a plan on how to deal with them.

My final recommendation is that practice should be respected.

Practice is a wonderful opportunity to improve and develop faster.

PRINCIPLE 4:
ADAPTABILITY

EVERYTHING CHANGES

Everything in life changes.

The only constant is change.

As we continue our career journeys' we will have to adapt and make changes.

If everything changes in our careers then so should we.

EMBRACE CHANGE

I completely understand that embracing change will be hard for some of us.

We may be reluctant to making changes and adapting.

I want to challenge you think of change as your good friend that is here to help you achieve your career goals.

Your friends are special to you.

You enjoy good times with them.

You can have the same experiences with change and adaptability.

You have to change your mindset first.

I am grateful that we have the opportunity to adapt in life.

Just imagine if our first attempts in life were permanent.

The world would be a different place.

JUDGMENTAL

Do not be so judgmental when it comes to adapting to changes.

Give change a chance before you become the judge, jury, and executioner.

When we judge prematurely we limit our growth and the possibilities available to us.

Harsh judgement delays dreams and goals.

VERY FORTUNATE

Humans are very fortunate.

We have the ability to adapt to our environment(s) and every day circumstances.

Adaptability is so instinctive to us.

We unconsciously forget that other species are not so fortunate.

Animals can adapt but only to their natural environments.

DON'T LEAVE ME

"Don't leave me."

This is a very emotional statement.

However, a majority of us are left daily when we do not adapt and change.

A common example of this occurs every day in the office when our management team wants us to complete a task.

Our typical response is "That is not my job. Why should I do it? What is in it for me?"

Adaptability will make sure that you don't miss the train but more importantly you can decide what seat you want to sit in.

NEW LESSONS AND EXPERIENCES ARE WAITING FOR YOU

Adaptability and changing will present us with new lessons and experiences.

If we say no to these opportunities we will never know what was waiting for us.

I can personally attest to learning new lessons and having different experiences because I was willing to adapt and change.

SKYROCKET POTENTIAL

Adapting and making changes in your career allows for your career to skyrocket and achieve the highest potential.

Change will be required to achieve your wildest dreams.

Majority of us do not like change.

If we do make the changes, they occur later than initially.

Adapting and making changes allow for our careers to grow like a rocket on a sunny afternoon.

I can personally confirm that I have witnessed and experienced growth in my career when I made changes and adapted to new situations.

PLANS GONE WRONG

To panic or not to panic that is the question?

We all make plans.

We believe the plans will go according to the way we envision them in our heads.

Unfortunately, life does not work that way.

Plans go wrong all the time.

How well do we respond when plans go wrong?

I strongly suggest you learn how to deal with plans going wrong because it will happen in your career.

We should anticipate something going wrong in our plans.

This anticipation will allow us to be ready for any surprises.

The chance of becoming angry with ourselves will decrease.

I know many people who want to quit on their dreams when their plans go wrong.

COMMON ACTION: ADAPTABILITY

"I don't like change."

"Why do I have to be the one that has to adapt?"

"Why can't this stay the same?"

You may not like change but it is recommended that you do it.

Making changes limit the probability of experiencing negative career results.

You don't have to adapt.

You can stay the same but life and your career industry will continue to change daily.

All career industries change.

RECOMMENDED ACTION: ADAPTABILITY

Change and adaptability are requirements for your career.

I suggest we invest in strategies and or additional resources to help cope with change and adaptability.

We do not have to face change and adaptability alone if it makes us uncomfortable initially.

PART II- ATTRACTION

WHAT IS ATTRACTION?

Attraction is a misunderstood word when it comes to our careers.

Most of us were never taught how attraction works.

Attraction is the process of having career opportunities appear in your life with little or no ease.

Some of us are told that if you want something you have to chase after it.

Chasing may be beneficial for some but it is better to attract career opportunities with half the effort and stress.

Entertainers and athletes are two groups who have experienced how attraction works.

Aspiring entertainers and athletes try to contact successful brands and inform them that they want to work with them.

The problem is most entertainers and athletes have achieved little to no results.

They finally decide to master their craft and attend industry events.

A representative from one of the successful brands contacts the entertainer or athlete for a meeting.

The rest can be history.

Literally history can be changed forever.

DOES ATTRACTION REALLY WORK?

If you ask successful people or high-income earners if attraction works, they will smile confirming that attraction does work.

I can personally attest that attraction works.

I have achieved certain career goals and milestones because of attraction.

Attraction has allowed me to meet mentors who pointed me in the right direction.

My mentors helped me achieve my goals in half the time with half the stress.

NO TIME FOR ATTRACTION, JUST GO FOR IT!

I completely understand that some of us may say that we have no time for attraction.

"I am just going to go for it."

"This approach has been successful for me producing satisfactory results so far."

Just going for it may be effective but attraction will accelerate the process.

In my opinion once you understand how attraction works you will want to use it daily to manifest your career goals.

Attraction has helped me in ways I could have never imagined.

I have been using attraction consistently for 6 years and the return on investment has been astronomical.

I have developed a professional brand at my current company and this all started by helping one person in a different division.

The ironic part about helping this individual is that I provided assistance because it was the right thing to do.

My intention was not to receive special recognition or rewards.

This experience has led to additional experiences and opportunities I never knew existed.

COMMON MISTAKES I DID NOT KNOW ABOUT

When we chase instead of attracting career opportunities, we make common mistakes.

Unfortunately, we are not aware that we are making these common mistakes.

Attraction when applied correctly can help reduce the common mistakes.

A common mistake we make is being over eager for a specific career opportunity.

MONEY CHASER

Some of us take pride in being a money chaser.

We have to prove to others that we are mighty and determined.

We believe we know how money works but the majority of us do not.

The truth is when you chase money you actually make money run from you.

Chasing money is an outward expression of desperation and you want to cure this money disease as soon as possible.

I have also been a victim of being a money chaser earlier in my career.

I was not happy with my job and I thought about quitting.

My goal was to look for another job.

I was chasing job after job going on interview after interview and not receiving job offers.

I analyzed why I was struggling.

The signs were obvious.

I was desperate and a money chaser.

No employer wanted to associate themselves with such an individual.

I completely understood.

Switching from money chaser to career attractor can be difficult at first but with time and practice just like almost any skill we can improve our results.

APPROPRIATE ATTRACTION

When attraction is applied appropriately to our careers, we will be amazed by what we can achieve.

There is a right and wrong way to do almost everything and career attraction is no different.

Another common mistake we make is being impatient.

We have this "microwave mindset".

We want immediate results.

 If the results do not taste great then we move on to the next strategy or shortcut.

ONE AT A TIME

We should develop our career one step at a time.

Every career opportunity should also be done one at a time.

Attempting to engage in more than one career opportunity at a time without the knowledge and experience will potentially lead to career disappointment.

Your career is a marathon.

I know we see certain "successful unicorns" in society that have achieved great wins in a short period of time.

Most of us will not be unicorns.

We need to just accept this.

We can all achieve great results in a long period of time.

I would challenge you to prove yourself one opportunity at a time.

Use each experience as a spring board to move to a higher level.

PRINCIPLE 5:
BRANDING

Most of us are familiar with branding when it comes businesses.

Brands express their values and beliefs.

However, professional and personal branding are mysterious for most of us.

Some business branding principles apply to us as well when it comes to our careers.

Branding is powerful in business no matter what level it is executed on.

You are branding yourself daily even if you are not aware of it.

BRANDING BASICS

There are branding basics when creating, developing, and maintaining a brand.

Who knows you?

This question is important.

When interacting with others they will have a positive or negative image of you.

If no one knows you are now is a good time to invest in building your brand.

Who do you want to become?

What is your goal?

Do you want to be the best in your industry?

Do you want to be the best at your company?

Do you want to be the best in your department or division?

Maybe you just want to come to work and do a great job and let your results do the talking.

We all have different motivations but we all need at least one.

My goal was to be the best in my department.

I had to work harder than everyone.

I started with a disadvantage.

I started 3 steps behind.

I turned a disadvantage into a competitive advantage.

What do other people say about you?

What type of reputation have you developed with people that constantly interact with you?

What others say about you matters.

Sometimes you may not be able to control the negative opinions others have about you.

Positive opinions should significantly outweigh negative opinions.

The most important question to ask is what do you say about you?

Self-esteem, self-image, and the words you speak to yourself will determine your confidence and results that you produce.

I call it personal internal marketing.

I recommend we become the most important marketer in our lives and careers.

What are your standards?

Standards and Values reign supreme and helps differentiate your brand from other brands.

BRANDING MISTAKE: POWER OF BUILDING A BRAND?

A common mistake we make is not understanding the power of building a brand while building a career.

The sad reality is that most workers in the marketplace are average.

Why would I mention such a statement?

Most of us show up to work late.

Leave on time.

Complete just enough work throughout the day to avoid being terminated.

This cycle becomes a self-fulfilling prophecy.

Once a career advancement opportunity arises, we are mad, angry, upset or a combination of all three that we were not considered for this opportunity.

The irony is that we make purchases every day with the brands that we love.

We never considered applying those same branding principles to achieving our career goals.

Build a brand and you will attract opportunities to you.

I have developed and built a huge career brand at my current company.

I achieved this unconsciously.

I was not aware of the principles that I executed.

I continue to utilize some of those same branding principles every day to maintain my professional brand.

BRANDING MISTAKE: BRAND IDENTITY?

Misunderstanding the power of a brand is a bad mistake.

Creating a bad brand identity is worse than not understanding the power of branding.

Who are you as a brand?

What do you stand for?

"Stand for nothing and fall for everything."

This adage is so true.

There are two common paths that lead to brand confusion or brand inconsistency.

The first path is understanding who we want to become.

We initially had strong values, principles, and standards.

Unfortunately, we receive career advancement in a corporate environment and yield to corporate politics.

The transition to corporate politician becomes real to protect career stability.

We fear retaliation from our superiors.

The second path is never developing an identity.

We will do anything to be liked.

We will say yes to everything with the expectation that our efforts will be rewarded.

Both paths are dangerous.

I personally believe that you should be your authentic self.

I understand this is a hard thing to do especially in career political environments.

However, I still strongly believe there are people who will appreciate and value you for the results that you can produce.

BRANDING MISTAKE: OVER COMPLICATION?

Another common branding mistake is over complication.

This branding mistake is also known as "analysis paralysis".

Brands are built one step at a time.

We can re-brand ourselves at any moment we chose.

Building a brand is not permanent.

We must take the necessary actions every day to build the brand we imagine.

I understand you may be thinking that you don't want to make mistakes.

We want to build a brand perfectly.

Newsflash every company brand has had to endure mistakes.

Mistakes occurred when companies were just starting and even when they started to growth.

We all overcomplicate things.

I recommend simplicity when it comes to brand building.

Your audience will thank you for it.

The most important thing is to just get started.

Life is a marathon.

Build your career brand until the day you decide to retire.

The decision is yours.

BRANDING MISTAKE: I WANT TO BE JUST LIKE YOU?

There is a time and place for learning from others.

Learn principles from others but maintain your identity.

We brand ourselves similar to others.

When we do this it becomes hard to differentiate between us and the people we want to be like.

I highly recommend we innovate ourselves if possible.

You are unique so embrace your personality.

Being unique may take longer to develop charisma with others.

However, the delayed time will be worth it in the long run.

"If you copy others then you will be a junior version of the original."

People will overlook you.

Why should people select you when they can go to the original source and get the results they seek?

BRANDING MISTAKE: SHINY OBJECT SYNDROME?

Shiny object syndrome became a common branding mistake in the early 2000's and continues today.

The shiny object syndrome is chasing after the latest trend or hack instead of remain committed and patient to your career plan.

I understand we need to make adjustments to our career plans based on marketplace activity and new technologies.

A great example is you love real estate and pursue a career in real estate.

You will experience difficult challenges in real estate.

Some friends tell you about block chain and cryptocurrencies.

"Block chain is going to be huge and you need to take advantage of this opportunity."

You agree and start to pursue block chain and cryptocurrencies but two problems exist.

Number one you really have no passion or significant interest in this industry.

You don't learn as much as you can.

You become average just like the rest of the investors who have recently invested in this.

Number two all markets and industries have low points and risks.

You lose a substantial amount of money and now you are angry.

You have been a victim of the shiny object syndrome.

Remaining committed with real estate and being patient could have avoided this career frustration.

I believe we should participate in an industry that we love.

When we do knowledge increases allowing us to weather career thunderstorms.

COMMON ACTION: BRANDING

We focus on short term rewards potentially affecting long term rewards.

Long term rewards can be worth the wait.

Impatience run rampant in our career because we want results immediately.

"I have to do this one thing right now and this way."

RECOMMENDED ACTION: BRANDING

I recommend taking a step back and thinking about everything carefully.

Understand how every action you take will affect future steps and the career goals that you want to accomplish.

I know it may be hard to believe an experience that occurred 5 years in the past will be connected to an experience 15 years in the future.

I advocate that we be strategic in our approach when it comes to building a brand.

PRINCIPLE 6: MARKETING

WORLDWIDE BROADCAST

Marketing is essentially broadcasting to the world a specific message you want the world to know about.

I know most of us do not view marketing as broadcasting.

Marketing is viewed as mysterious or taboo.

Especially if we are not good at marketing our message.

Your broadcast can now be worldwide with the help of the internet and social media marketing.

Since we have access to a worldwide audience, we should make sure our marketing and messaging is meaningful and connects with our ideal audience.

We will increase the quality of life by adding value or solving a problem.

MARKETING ACTION STEPS

Every step that you take is a marketing message broadcasted to your ideal audience.

If you show up to work late frequently you are broadcasting to your superiors and your team you are not serious about your work.

You are unpredictable.

You can't be trusted with certain projects because you can't even show up to work on time.

You mismanage your day with distractions when you are at work.

Once again you are broadcasting that you most likely will not meet important deadlines.

SHORT TERM VS LONG TERM MARKETING

Based on personal experiences I prefer long-term results over short-term results.

In the past I was just like most people focused on the short-term results and not the long-term results.

My long-term results were not the best because my short-term results sabotaged them.

Marketing should be viewed as a marathon and not a quick sprint.

Short-term marketing needs the same tender loving care that long-term marketing does.

Short-term and long-term marketing should have different marketing strategies applied to them to be the most effective.

In the short-term we should market ourselves as a results maker.

Someone who adds value to others.

Also, a person who is open to career collaborations.

In the long-term focus on your vision, the big goals, and the best way to market your vision and goals to potential marketing partners and the marketplace.

PRODUCT MARKETING

Shocking revelation the product is the marketing.

You are the product.

I understand that this can be confusing.

We should strive to deliver a great product to the marketplace.

Product marketing is very prevalent in Silicon Valley.

Silicon Valley presents limited marketing and advertising messages to promote a new product.

The product is delivered and displayed to a small audience.

The product should be very persuasive as to why you should purchase the product.

Once I started viewing myself as a product and became conscious about my marketing, I began to see outstanding results.

I strongly believe if we all viewed ourselves as products our execution and results would be completely different.

We would not display and deliver poor results if we were scrutinized and rated as products are on a regular basis.

Would you purchase you as a product?

MARKETING P'S

Product, Price, Promotion, Place/People.

Each of the four has a different mindset that I want us to think about.

During the product phase we should be focused on development.

Ensuring we are making the best product we possibly can.

I advocate investing hours, months, and years in your career development.

The most growth always comes from the most investment and development.

Product affects price in a major way.

During the price phase you will be evaluated based on the value you add to others and the marketplace.

The more value you can add to the marketplace the higher you can sell your product.

We all know that value is usually associated with price.

High value tends to yield high price.

Hotels are the prime example of value to price connection.

When I lodge at a luxury resort the experience, value, and price are completely different than a standard hotel that provides the basics.

The choice is yours.

You have several options from an economy motel to a luxury resort.

My desire is to become the best "luxury resort" that I can be.

I want to make my guest happy so that they return to the resort on a frequent basis.

During the promotion phase focus on the amount of times you are able to display your marketing to your ideal audience.

Do not over promote.

Over promotion can lead to diluting your brand and marketing due to overexposure.

Do not under promote as well.

Under promotion will make it harder to build an emotional connection with the audience.

The audience would not have enough time to make a decision on whether they want to purchase your product or not.

This balancing act will take time, practice, and patience.

During the place and people phases different places and people require different strategies.

Unfortunately, we do not apply different strategies to different people and places.

We become lazy and use the same strategies at different places and with different people.

The marketing mystery arrives.

We wonder why the execution was poor and the results were lackluster at best.

I beg you don't make the fatal mistake of being last and treating each place and person the same.

MARKETING MISTAKE: CONFUSING STRATEGIES AND TACTICS

A simple and easy marketing mistake made frequently is confusing strategies with tactics.

A strategy is focused on the vision of obtaining a certain goal.

Strategies are primarily based on principles and psychology.

Strategies are usually timeless no matter the tactics.

Tactics are based on the practical application on how to achieve your vision or goal in the shortest amount of time.

There is a big difference between the two.

Strategies are usually long-term and require easy integration.

Tactics can change all the time.

We love headlines that mention the latest tactic or trick only setting us up for disappointment.

Let's use the concept of this book to display the difference between the two.

My goal in this book as promised in the subtitle is to help you achieve more money in half the time with half the stress.

A tactical person would spend all day searching online for the latest and greatest tactics to execute on their audience.

A strategist will focus on the goal they want to accomplish and strategically work backwards on effectively executing the necessary steps that will increase the probability of achieving the goal.

Tactical people generally tend to be focused on their needs and wants.

They chase money as we mentioned earlier.

You should not do this.

Strategists' strive to add value to people.

Strategists' understand that goal achievement is a long-term process.

Strategies focus on adding value and developing relationships with the "sub-audience" first and then the "main audience."

The sub-audience gets overlooked and can be the difference between you achieving your goal or not.

For example, you want to work for your dream company and as a tactical person you want to reach the Senior Vice President of your ideal dream division.

You listen to other tactical people informing you about the best tactics to get the Senior Vice President's attention and interest in you.

After months of hard work and effort with no results the tactical person becomes frustrated and quits their pursuit to reach the Senior Vice President.

The strategist works their way up the corporate chain of command.

The strategist starts to develop a relationship with the internal mail associate who delivers mail to all the employees at the company.

You become good friends with the mail associate who introduces who to some secretaries.

The secretaries introduce you to managers.

Managers make introductions to the Senior Vice President's secretary.

You develop a relationship with the Senior Vice President's secretary and you get the meeting that you always wanted.

Do you see the difference in execution?

Relationships are still powerful and important to achieving your goals.

MARKETING MISTAKE: LACK OF CONSISTENCY

We currently have a 24/7 lifestyle.

We need to market consistently in our careers.

We should strive to always update ourselves especially when it comes to our minds and career execution.

Some people have a year 2000 mindset and execution but we are in 2018.

Obviously, this is a problem.

Initially we want to be the president and or CEO of a successful company.

Next week we want to be an entrepreneur that will impact the world.

The following week we are real estate investors.

Our lack of consistency confuses our audiences.

We also become confused in the process.

I recommend we make a conscious effort to market consistency.

MARKETING MISTAKE: ME MARKETING (AUDIENCE MOTIVATION?)

A terrible mistake we all make or have made in our careers is the concept of "me marketing".

"Me marketing" is exactly what it means.

We are only concerned about the marketing message we can present to our audience.

We believe this will help us get what we want from them.

Stop this marketing mistake immediately.

We should place a greater focus on our audience's motivation.

What does my audience care about the most?

How can I resolve or assist in resolving their current issue?

How can I add immense value to them?

MARKETING MISTAKE: REACHING THE WRONG AUDIENCE

A simple marketing mistake that can easily be avoided or limited is reaching the wrong audience.

Newsflash everyone is not your audience to present your marketing message to.

You are not a multi-national corporation that can spend millions of dollars on a television advertisement to the entire country.

The television advertisement will most likely be seen by only 50% of the country.

15 % of the country will remember the marketing of your television advertisement.

Find your audience and stick to them like glue.

Most of us are worried that our audience is too small and want massive awareness initially.

Marketing insight: market to smaller audiences first and then market out to larger audiences.

Your marketing should be convincing and engaging to smaller audiences.

Smaller audiences will tell larger audiences about your marketing.

Word-of-mouth marketing will be active.

Word-of-mouth marketing is very powerful.

Some of the biggest brands in the world became successful financially and socially because of word-of-mouth marketing.

MARKETING MISTAKE: MAKING ASSUMPTIONS

The wrong marketing assumptions can lead to wrong results.

We all are guilty of this.

We make assumptions about what we think our audience wants to see or need.

A good marketing recommendation is to ask your audience directly what they want or need.

An alternative approach would be to watch their behavior also known as buyer behavior.

We are creatures of habit.

Behavior says a lot about a person whether they are aware of it or not.

There is a possibility that sometimes your assumptions are right.

However, a better strategy would be to execute one of the previous strategies mentioned.

COMMON ACTION: MARKETING

Executing marketing activities similar to others is common.

The mindset is believing in the concept of safety in numbers.

Safety in numbers is based on the assumption that if a majority is engaging in certain activities we should do it too.

Safety in numbers also leads to social proof.

Social proof is that the majority can't be wrong in their thinking.

Unfortunately, the majority can be wrong in thinking just like the minority.

When it comes to marketing your career avoid this like the plague.

The cousin of similar marketing is throw-it-to-the wall.

You try any and every marketing tactic you can think of.

You also try marketing tactics advised to you.

The problem is we waste time, effort, and energy when we throw-it-to-the wall.

The time, effort, and energy could have been used in more beneficial ways.

Another fatal marketing mistake is "unconscious marketing".

We believe that a specific marketing resource or strategy is not real important until after further investigation.

Your hypothesis was incorrect.

RECOMMENDED ACTION: MARKETING

I strongly recommend getting clarity on your career goals.

Learn from others who have achieved what want to achieve.

Focus on strategy and planning instead of always executing.

Execution is an important component of achievement.

Having the right strategy will differentiate between achieving your goals and achieving your goals 10 times faster.

Quality is just as important if not more important than quantity.

Remain patient when you are just starting to build your marketing arsenal.

PRINCIPLE 7:
NETWORKING

NETWORTH IS NETWORK

Developing and maintaining a network is very important for our careers.

"Your network is your net worth."

There is truth in that statement.

The amount of money you make in your career will be in the direct proportion to the relationships and networks you currently have.

Based on my personal experience the career network that I have built has led to amazing career development and growth.

"People love to associate with people that they know, like, and trust."

Take the necessary time to grow your network to grow your net worth.

Networks grant you access.

People outside the network are denied access.

DEVELOP YOUR NETWORK

How do I develop my network?

The answer is simple but not easy.

We can develop our networks the same way we build any relationship-emotional connection.

There are two powerful but time-consuming ways to develop your network.

 Produce great results.

Add tremendous value to others.

10X NETWORK

 Networks help us achieve our goals 10X faster than attempting to achieve them on our own.

Do not stay in your comfort zone.

Expanding your zone will expand your network.

"Who you know is very important!"

AUTHENTIC NETWORKING

Always remember that you are unique.

No one can be you.

When networking do not try to become someone you are not.

Be authentic.

We are all emotional creatures.

Networkers know when something is not right.

In the past when I was networking my insecurities and image of inadequacy prevented me from being my authentic self.

I was concerned others would judge me unfairly.

This negative thought was only in my head.

I wanted to make a great first impression instead of being my authentic self.

At a past networking event I was myself and developed great new relationships.

CONFIDENTIAL DISPLAY

Display confidence when interacting with others.

I recommend that you remain calm the best that you can.

Do not try too hard to impress others.

You are nervous and so are they.

Let the interaction flow naturally instead of attempting to control it.

NETWORKING SECRET

A great networking secret is to be genuinely curious about others.

You goal is to get to know others better.

All of us love to talk about ourselves.

Push the right buttons and we will open up and connect.

NETWORKING MISTAKE: UNDERSTIMATING FACE-TO-FACE INTERACTION

We live in a hyper connected technological society.

We underestimate face-to-face interaction with others.

The advantage of meeting face-to-face is so we can make quick adjustments by observing a person's body language.

Go out and make great networking connections face-to-face.

Introverts hate networking because they have to be social with others.

Introverts I recommend talking with one person or two people when networking.

NETWORKING MISTAKE: NETWORKING IS A WASTE OF TIME?

Some people believe this next statement to be true.

"Networking is a waste of time!"

In my opinion most of us say or think this because we do not understand the benefits of networking.

I held this false belief also.

I knew that I was not naturally good at networking with others.

I assumed I was going to fail.

I wanted to avoid the failure.

I would tell myself that networking was a waste of time.

There have been times when initially I did not want go to a networking event.

At the end of the networking event I was glad that I attended.

I was introduced to new people.

New opportunities were presented to me because of the introductions.

We make a huge mistake believing that everyone we know will help us achieve our career goals.

Meeting new people and expanding our networks will help us achieve our career goals.

NETWORKING MISTAKE: SOCIAL MEDIA NETWORKING STRATEGY?

Social media has been in existence for over a decade.

Some of us believe that we don't need a networking strategy for social media.

Believing you don't need a social media networking strategy will be a big networking mistake.

Our social media networking strategy should be focused on four main objectives.

1) Who is your audience?

2) Where does your audience appear on social media?

3) What does your audience care about?

4) How to add value to your audience?

There are still people who believe social media is a fad or not worth investing in.

The "social media fad" idea is based on a lack of understanding how social media actually works.

Impatience is another reason why social media is labeled as a fad.

Impatience comes from wanting an immediate return on investment due to short-term priorities.

I recommend creating social media accounts and keeping them active.

Engaging and entertaining content should be uploaded to your accounts frequently.

There are people making six figures from their social media networking and so can you.

NETWORKING MISTAKE: TAKING WITHOUT GIVING

A common networking mistake is taking without giving.

This mindset is focused on what I can get from others.

The focus should be what can I give to others?

We focus only on ourselves and forget about adding value to others.

I heard a story about two aspiring movie directors.

Two aspiring movie directors met a veteran movie director and producer.

Movie director number one spoke with the veteran and all he talked about was the movie he wanted to make.

He was only concerned with how the veteran could help him.

This conversation went from bad to worse.

Movie director number one spoke about 98% of the time during the conversation.

He was dismissed.

Movie director number two was a fan.

She was curious about how the veteran created one of her favorite scenes in one of the veteran's movies.

The veteran was impressed with movie director number two.

He asked her if she was working on any projects.

She said yes.

He gave her his card and told her to send a copy of the project to him.

She sent the screenplay to him and he helped her make her first movie.

He has become her mentor.

They are developing several projects together.

The lesson is to focus on others and they will help you in the future.

NETWORKING MISTAKE: TALKING 2X MORE THAN LISTENING

This networking mistake goes hand and hand with taking without giving.

We are so self-centered.

We talk twice as much as we listen.

We all like to talk about ourselves.

We also love when others listen to what we have to say.

The goal is create a balance between talking and listening.

A great networking secret is to flip these proportions.

Listen twice and much as you talk and your conversations will be more intriguing.

Create this intrigue and others will want to know more about you.

COMMON ACTION: NETWORKING

A common networking philosophy is believing networking is all about taking from others.

This philosophy is supposed to help us accomplish our career goals in the fastest time possible.

Based on the examples previously mentioned you will notice that when changing the focus from yourself to others great things start to manifest.

RECOMMENDED ACTION: NETWORKING

I strongly recommend we continue to work hard in private but also network effectively.

Place the spotlight on others because people love to talk about themselves.

Think about how you can add value or solve a problem for others.

Helping others will increase the probability that they will be more open to helping you as well.

This is known as the law of reciprocity.

PRINCIPLE 8: ADVERTISING

WALKING BILLBOARD

Have you ever heard the saying "You are a walking billboard"?.

There is truth in that statement.

The reason is wherever you go you are advertising.

Your actions are a reflection of your dominant internal thoughts.

SELECTIVE MESSAGING

The good news about being a billboard is that we get to choose the messaging.

With this power we can change the messaging anytime we want.

Your messaging should be a combination of four criteria

1) Authentic to you
2) Your beliefs
3) Your passions
4) Your audience interests.

Bad messaging is creating advertisements you do not feel passionate about it.

The message will not resonate with your audience.

SELECTIVE AUDIENCE

Similar to selective messaging you can also select your audience to advertise to.

Delivering the right message to the right audience is crucial in life and in your career.

Sometimes we have to change our audience initially but later in our careers we can re-target that same audience.

ENGAGING ADVERTISING

Engaging advertising attempts to stimulate the emotions.

The goal is to develop a deep connection with the audience.

Persuasion is also included in the mix to enhance the effectiveness of the advertisement.

Ultimately after persuasion has done its job influence and impact round out the trio to ensure the audience is captivated.

ENTERTAINMENT ADVERTISING

Entertainment advertising is the most common.

In the past entertainment advertising was the best.

Entertainment advertising provides the element of fun.

We love to have fun.

Fun is the reason why so many of us are distracted with entertaining content on a daily basis.

EDUCATIONAL ADVERSTISING

Educational advertising is not as well-known as engaging and entertaining advertising.

Educational advertising was initially intended to provide knowledge to the audience.

Audiences believed educational advertisements to be boring and a waste of time.

We avoided them as much as we could.

Around 2004 audiences became more curious about life.

We craved progress.

Advertisers changed their education advertising from knowledge to aspirational providing inspiration and insight into what is actually possible.

ADVERTISING CAMPAIGNS

I want you to consider yourself as an advertiser.

You are an advertiser for your career.

We are constantly advertising.

Advertising campaigns consist of: ads, sequencing, messaging, timing, results, and sales.

Ads are focused on a specific goal.

What do we want to accomplish with this ad?

Do we want to increase our brand awareness with this ad(s)?

Do we want to increase the sales of a specific product or service?

Sequencing is important.

Our ads should be in chronological order.

Our advertising strategy should create curiosity and intrigue.

Messaging is what do want to say to your audience?

Timing is also important.

If the product or service is seasonal and executed at the wrong time it can lead to a disaster.

The results will be wasted time, effort, and energy.

What metrics are currently in place to track the results of the ad?

How do you know if the ad was just a test, a success, or a failure?

Failure can lead to a learning experience.

Lastly, how many customers purchased the product or service?

What was the total revenue generated from the ad?

WORD OF MOUTH ADVERTISING

A great boost to your career is word of mouth advertising and the third party validation from others.

Word of mouth advertising can be positive and negative depending on the experience others have with you.

I have built my career unconsciously on word of mouth advertising.

This was never my intention.

My two primary goals were to complete the current task and be a hard worker.

My results are the by product from focusing on my two primary goals.

ADVERTISING MISTAKE: NO ADVERTISING PLAN OR STRATEGY

What is your advertising plan or strategy for your career?

The response will be confused looks on faces.

There are two reasons for this reaction.

We don't have an advertising plan.

We haven't even thought about it.

It never crossed our minds.

I understand we did not attend a course called Career Advertising 101.

We should all have advertising plans or strategies.

The most successful retailers have advertising plans and strategies to increase the probability for achieving their desirable results.

We can learn advertising lessons from the retailers.

ADVERTISING MISTAKE: MISS-MANGAGING THE ADVERTISING BUDGET

Advertising expenses that are miss-managed effects the remaining potential expenses in the budget.

A common reason for the miss management is betting a huge majority of the advertising budget on a single advertising campaign.

Advertising expenses should have been allocated for multiple advertising campaigns.

For example allocating advertising expenses toward our outward appearance for clothing, shoes, and accessories.

Advertising expenses for our inner appearance such as learning new things and networking with others are non-existent or minimal.

There are times when betting big on one premier advertising campaign is beneficial and rewarding.

We must be willing to accept the consequences if the campaign is not executed as initially envisioned.

ADVERTISING MISTAKE: FOCUS ON SELLING INSTEAD OF CONNECTING FIRST

This is a huge problem with advertisers and marketers.

We are constantly selling instead of connecting with our audience.

We are so focused on the short-term results because of some high pressure goal(s).

We believe that every time we see our audience that we should present something for sale to them.

I understand there may be a small percentage of the audience who needs what you are trying to sell right now.

I recommend we always connect first and then transition into the sale instead of the common traditional approach.

Buy my product. Buy my product. Buy my product.

We are inundated with marketing and sales messages 24/7.

The internet does not sleep.

We can reach almost any of the 7.7 billion people on the planet.

Provide value to your audience 3 times before you ask them to purchase your product, service, or donate to your cause.

I can personally say that the 3-to-1 approach works.

If an advertiser or marketer were to implement this strategy more sales would increase.

We would purchase their products and services more.

Most companies will not execute the 3-to-1 strategy because they just want to meet a sales goal.

Companies will resort to becoming transactional instead of being patient and building a relationship with us.

I am also a marketer.

I continue to study marketing psychology and buyer behavior.

ADVERTISING MISTAKE: RIGHT PRODUCT, WRONG TIMING

This next advertising mistake can be damaging to any advertiser.

Right product wrong time.

This usually happens for one of two reasons.

The product or service is seasonal.

Out of season.

Our audience knows this and are willing to wait for the correct season to appear.

The audience is willing to purchase the product or service out of season but the advertiser is not willing to offer the product or service.

We have to be very careful when dealing with seasonal products and services.

How many times have we seen an entertainment artist not understand the season they are in?

We decide to quit on the entertainment dream.

We did not see the progress we were looking for.

We did not understood the current season we are in.

We could have made the necessary adjustments.

ADVERTISING MISTAKE: WRONG DISTRIBUTION CHANNEL

Another frustrating advertising mistake is not understanding the proper distribution channel.

The advertising message is good but the wrong medium was chosen.

The audience does not respond the way they should.

Every distribution channel and medium has its own native language, standards, and requirements.

An example would be creating a TV ad when the proper advertising should have been a news publication.

Social media platforms also have their own native language for communicating with others.

Advertisers will upload or insert videos on a written distribution channel.

A written publication will be uploaded or inserted on a video distribution channel.

Understanding distribution helps us communicate and advertise.

Create for the appropriate channel to obtain the best results.

COMMON ACTION: ADVERTISING

Short and simple we do not take advertising seriously.

We believe career advertising is confusing.

Successful and high performers understand career advertising.

We are disconnected with career advertising.

Career Advertising was not taught to the masses.

Out of sight.

Out of mind.

We are not thoughtful and mindful about advertising messages displayed to our audiences.

Thinking about our decisions and actions can be troublesome.

Being thoughtful and mindful can be done slowly over time.

The more practice we get the better we will be.

RECOMMENDED ACTION: ADVERTISING

Just be human.

Be your natural and authentic self.

Add an element of emotion.

Don't worry about being perfect.

Genuinely attempt to help others.

Work on advertising effectively.

You can advertise your way to your career goals.

PART III – EXECUTION

YOUR MOMENT HAS ARRIVED

The moment you have been waiting for is finally here.

All of your previous hard work has led to this.

Make sure to take advantage of your moment.

ULTIMATE SEPARATOR

Execution is the ultimate separator between the high-income earners and everyone else.

EXECUTION OF STRATEGY

Execution of strategy is important.

Execution itself is not enough.

There are a lot of us that execute everyday but the results are highly different.

PRINCIPLE 9: FOCUS

FOCUS EXPANDS

Whatever your mind focuses on will expand leading to a positive or negative experience

This is a profound statement.

Simplicity in nature.

There is truth displayed in the statement.

The problem is that we tend to focus on minor things instead of major things.

Focus on the positive and positive will appear.

Focus on the negative and negative will appear.

FOCUS ON THE GOAL

Focus on the goal that you are attempting to achieve.

This is easier said than done.

Focus requires sacrifice and saying no.

Focusing on why you want to achieve the goal will help you achieve the goal.

A strong motivation for why the goal is important to you will help you preserve to accomplish the goal.

As I write these words, I am focusing on why I want to write this book.

I usually write in the morning.

I am writing to you in the afternoon.

I had to make some personal changes to my schedule today.

I am aware that writing in the afternoon will not produce my best work.

However, I do not want break the momentum of writing every day.

Average writing is better than not writing at all.

I decided to write in the afternoon no matter the outcome.

I am focused on writing a great book for you.

I want this book to impact your life.

I want to deliver on my promise in the substile for this book.

"Making more money in half the time with half the stress."

Writing a book is overdue.

I should have written a book years ago.

I am determined to complete this book in the shortest amount of time.

REDUCE AND OR ELIMINATE DISTRACTIONS

Distractions are the enemies of productivity.

Distractions have become a part of life.

We engage with distractions on a daily basis.

Some distractions are small and others are big.

Distractions can be painful.

We waste large amounts of time.

Once the time is gone it is gone.

I strongly recommend that you eliminate distractions completely.

Eliminating distractions may be harsh.

Doing this will make your life better.

Happiness and fulfillment are waiting for you on the other side.

If you can't eliminate distractions then reduce them in your everyday life.

Committing to a schedule will help eliminate and reduce distractions.

As I mentioned above, I write in the morning.

My family knows that in the early morning I need to write.

During this time, I am my best.

POWER OF SCHEDULE

There is power in a schedule.

You get a head start while others are trying to determine what they want to engage their time in.

This is so true.

Priorities are placed on the schedule.

A schedule informs you what needs to get done for the day.

A lack of schedule will increase your distraction time.

Distraction time increases the probability of wasting the whole day on low level activities.

After further investigation we will be mad with ourselves.

We did not accomplish what we needed to do.

What about having fun?

Fun can be scheduled as well.

Scheduling helps us stay focused and increases the probability that the important activities will be completed by their deadlines.

Once a schedule has been created, we need to stick to it as much as we can.

A schedule is a guide and there will be times when you can't execute according to the schedule.

Make the necessary adjustments when the schedule needs to be changed.

Actions become habits.

Television programs and entertainment events have schedules.

You must follow the schedule to enjoy the television programs and entertainment events.

We have no problem following a schedule when it comes to certain areas of our lives but others are neglected consistently.

IMPORTANCE OF SELF-DISCIPLINE

Distractions and other activities make self-discipline hard to practice.

Self-discipline should be viewed as a trusted advisor that helps you achieve your goals, needs, and wants.

After execution self-discipline is required to achieve your career dreams and live the life you want.

There are videos on the internet talking about the importance of self-discipline.

Self-discipline grants access to having almost anything that you want.

Self-discipline has two important requirements: sacrifice and suffering.

Self-discipline requires we sacrifice our current wants for future wants.

When developing self-discipline, you will suffer.

Perseverance is needed when it gets hard.

HARDEST WORD TO SAY (NO)

No is the hardest word to say.

No means we are unable participate in a particular activity.

Unfortunately, we should not say yes to everything.

There will be times when you have to say no.

Maybe you want to start a business or pursue a passion project.

You will need to devote extra hours to make that business or passion project a reality.

Saying yes to the business and passion project means saying no to family and friends.

I have said no to family and friends because completing this book is very important.

Telling others, no or having an accountability partner that will increase focus and results.

FOCUS CREATES CLARITY

Clarity is one of the most underappreciated habits.

Clarity is powerful.

Clarity is similar to eye vision.

Our vision is very important to our eyes.

We make decisions with our eyes every day.

"We are visual creatures."

If our vision (clarity) is so important why don't we develop it more?

Self-discipline, dedication, and commitment is required to develop anything.

We make decisions based on how far we think see.

This is also the reason why most parents advocate for their children to pursue careers in professional services and STEM (Science, Technology, Engineering, and Mathematics).

The clarity is very high for these careers whereas Entertainment Arts (Painter, Recording Artist, Actor, and Creative Writing) is not.

There are so many variable components where the career path is not laid out completely.

Entertainment arts requires you to have faith.

We must continue to make progress one step at a time.

Remain confident that everything will work out for the best.

Increase discipline and so will focus and clarity.

Clarity increases your confidence.

High confidence allows us to overcome challenges along the way.

We will arrive at our desired career destinations.

COMMON ACTION: FOCUS

Too many of us have low levels of focus.

I believe the reason for this is because focus requires saying no to other activities.

We believe that by saying no we are missing out on potential fun activities.

We are easily distracted.

For example, you want to work a special project or research something that interest you.

10 minutes into your focus time someone contacts you.

You receive an invitation to go somewhere with them.

80% of us will say yes.

Invitation accepted.

We focus on minor activities instead of major activities.

We ask ourselves "How did I get here?

"Why did this happen to me?"

We all know the answers to these questions.

We produced unsatisfactory results.

RECOMMENDED ACTION: FOCUS

I recommend developing an intense focus.

How do I do that?

One step at a time.

Determine the focus for every activity you engage in.

My family and friends will want to spend recreation time with me.

I would love to.

However my immediate focus is on completing this book.

Once the book is completed I will have to shift by focus to marketing this book.

Focus is power.

Power produces productive results.

PRINCIPLE 10: TEAMWORK

TEAMS PRODUCE OUTSTANDING RESULTS

We focus on one individual producing results.

Teamwork produces outstanding results.

The group should share the credit when the results are great and when they are bad.

The truth is that life is a team game and so is your career.

All successful people and high-income earners know this.

He or she who has the best team wins.

Silicon Valley understands the importance of team work.

I believe this is the reason why so many great companies are present in that business ecosystem.

Employees in the "Valley" want to be "lifers".

Lifer means that employees love the culture and career environment.

Their present employer has invested in them.

Employees have made conscious decisions to finish their career with this employer.

NOTHING IS ACCOMPLISHED ALONE

The best way to achieve optimal results is through synergetic collaboration.

Synergic Collaboration means all the members on the team understand how important they are to the team's success.

Our goal is to work together for the greater good of everyone.

We all know the story about the lone wolf and other animals that hunt alone.

Animals that hunt together have the highest chance of survival.

Nothing is accomplished alone.

Plants need water and the sun for photosynthesis.

There are multiple components that comprise what we know as "nature".

You are not achieving your career goals as fast as you like because you do not have enough help from others.

This happens for two reasons.

Analysis paralysis.

We over think everything.

We do not know where to start to ask for help.

The second reason could be that we know we need help but are not willing to ask for help because of our insecurities.

We falsely believe that others will perceive us to be weak if we ask for help.

TEAM STRENGTHS

Everyone can't be good at everything.

Everyone on the team can be good at something.

Together we can accomplish almost anything.

Unfortunately, throughout our life we have been told that we need to focus on our weakness.

I believe we should develop our strengths to maximum capacity.

Collaborate with others who are strong in your weakness.

The team collectively should compensate for all the weakness.

Team members should avoid becoming jealous of each other.

Do not compare yourself.

Everyone on the team is needed.

We all bring something special to the table.

As a team our focus needs to be collaboration not competition.

When we collaborate effectively, we all win together instead of struggling individually.

RECIPROCITY IN MOTION

I believe in the law of reciprocity.

Give to others and they are more likely to give to you in the same capacity.

I help you win.

You help me win.

Together we both win.

I look back on my career and see this law present.

At the time I did not know what this law was or called.

I would help others just because I believe that is the right thing to do.

When I needed a favor from these individuals, they were willing to help me.

My hope is that this book will provide value to you.

Maybe in the future when I need help you are able to help.

COMMON ACTION: TEAMWORK

We all have a tendency to want to do and or control everything.

We believe everything falls and rise underneath us.

Newsflash your knowledge and time is limited.

In addition you rob others the opportunity to help you and to become a part of history.

RECOMMENDED ACTION: TEAMWORK

I recommend we devote an enormous amount of time to focusing on our strengths.

Embrace collaboration to achieve your career goals at the speed of light.

Nothing in this world was created to be alone so do not become an island.

PRINCIPLE 11: EXPERIENCE

NEW EXPERIENCES

I strongly believe in being open to new experiences.

Saying yes to these experiences can open doors you never thought were possible.

I know that has been true for me.

This can become a habit.

Volunteering for new experiences will make you a high priority on another person's list.

When they need assistance, you will be requested to provide the necessary assistance.

New experiences help with the attraction section mentioned previously.

Your brand will can become influential.

Your marketing can be engaging.

Advertising is stellar.

A master networker.

"How do I open doors for my career?"

Say yes.

Always be willing to complete the small actions to prepare you for the big stage.

WORKING DURING A HURRICANCE

Earlier in my career I was working at a gas station.

The employees of one of our southern stores decided to close the store.

They decided to make this conscious decision without consulting with anyone but themselves.

Their management could not be reached.

My store received a phone call asking if anyone would be willing to cover the store overnight.

My trainer Jay Chandler volunteer.

Jay asked me if I was willing to go with him to cover the store.

Initially I was hesitant.

I was already working my normal shift.

I was looking forward to going home and relaxing.

I thought about it further and I agreed to join Jay on our "southern adventure".

We headed south and arrived at the store.

The store was a mess.

Literally.

Most of the store operations were not complete.

I was upset.

Jay saw opportunity.

I was wondering if I would regret this experience.

Jay: What store operations do you know?

JS: Well not much. I usually just sweep and clean.

Jay: All of that changes tonight.

JS: What do you mean?

Jay: I am going to train you tonight.

JS: What are we training on?

Jay: The cash register.

I was scared of the cash register because there were so many transactions and I had no practice.

JS: I don't know about the cash register. I think I will be terrible at it.

Jay: We got all night. I know you might be scared of it. I will be right here to guide you.

JS: Ok. Let's do it.

Jay and I clean the store first.

Next, we tackled the store reports.

He broke everything down so I could understand.

Jay explained the psychology of why we do what we do.

He also taught me managerial store operations that should have been restricted to me.

The moment finally came.

Cash register training.

I practiced a lot.

There were times when I wanted to quit learning the cash register.

Jay encouraged me.

He gave me feedback.

I made the necessary adjustments.

My confidence slowly started to increase dramatically.

Jay also trained me on the advance cash register transactions.

The sun raised and morning was upon us.

The next shift was about to start.

Time was up.

I was just starting to have fun.

I wanted more time at the store.

Jay and I left and headed back north.

We arrived back at my store.

My team members wanted to know about the experience.

Jay and I downplayed it.

Days later my management gave me a cash register to operate.

I was ready and wanted to show off the training that Jay gave me.

I was flying through the transactions.

Everybody was amazed by my production.

Stacy (Assistant Manager): Are you ok?

JS: Yes. Why do you ask?

Stacy: I am confused.

JS: Why?

Stacy: A few days ago, you were still afraid to operate the cash register and now you have become a "little master."

JS: I don't know what you are talking about.

Stacy: Don't play with me. We all noticed the difference.

JS: I finally got cash register training.

Stacy: Oh really? When?

JS: The other night when the hurricane hit.

Stacy: I thought you went home.

JS: No I went to the southern store.

Stacy: Which manager went with you?

JS: I was there with Jay.

Stacy: Oh. Now it makes sense.

Jay started at the company a few months before me and was promoted to trainer.

He became known for training new associates in record time.

I was living proof of this.

I am glad I volunteered for the "southern hurricane experience."

After the southern hurricane experience, I started to learn even more at a record paste.

I eventually became a back-up manager.

I could have become a full-time manager but scheduling conflicts permitted.

CASE MANAGEMENT OPPORTUNITY

I was very fortunate at an early age.

My mother helped me get a job at age 17.

I was now working with her at a health insurance company.

I was working with the Case Management department.

Nikki Lawson was the Manager for the department.

Nikki was a great person to work for.

She was always positive.

Nikki: Are you going straight home?

JS: No.

Nikki: I need help with a small project. Are you able to help?

JS: Sure.

Nikki taught me about the first and third trimesters when women are pregnant.

This was an eye-opening experience.

I learned so much.

Nikki's director was pleased with our collaboration and the results for the project.

He bought Nikki and I lunch on Friday.

He personally delivered the food.

Nikki personally introduced me to him.

He told me that if I need anything his door was open.

A few weeks later he invited me to his office to talk.

I accepted the invitation.

We started to develop a mentorship.

I learned a lot from him.

SUBJECT MATTER EXPERT

6 years ago, I started a new journey in the financial services industry.

I was recovering from a two-year mild depression.

I was given a new opportunity.

I may have mentioned this before.

This new opportunity gave me new life and I wanted to take advantage of it.

My management team had no expectations for me.

I wanted to be the best associate in my department.

In order to be the best, I knew I had to deliver results and consistently.

I set two goals.

Outlearn everyone.

Outwork everyone.

I have kept my promise to this day.

My senior manager at the time had more work than time to complete it.

I was hungry.

I was willing to help.

Nancy: Do you know about process 2?

JS: No

I didn't even know about process 1.

I was only responsible for mailing documents for process 1.

Nancy: Ok.

JS: If you teach me, I am willing to help.

Nancy's eyes lit up like July 4th fireworks.

Nancy: I will teach you.

So, the training began.

Nancy trained me on everything she possibly could.

I moved up the departmental ranks quickly in a short period of time.

Upper management was curious why a new hire was working so many hours.

Jason Fergerson was Nancy's superior.

Jason: Why is he [Joe] staying late and working so many hours?

Nancy: I have so much work that needs to be completed and he is the only one that wants to stay and help.

Jason became silent.

Nancy and I began working late nights.

I thought to myself.

"Nancy and Jason are going to kick me out the building for working so hard before I leave."

Nancy and I would work until 11:00pm at night Monday thru Thursday.

We would leave at 6pm on Friday.

Fast forward to today I still strive to outlearn everyone and outwork everyone.

I have become one of the most requested people to resolve escalated issues.

MEMORABLE EXPERIENCES

Create memorable experiences for others.

The people that you interact with should become brand ambassadors.

I have done this continuously on an unconscious level.

I want to do the best I can to help others.

I strive to give them the experience of a lifetime.

Creating positive memorable experiences will have people in amazement.

They will be shocked that they had an amazing experience with you.

EXECUTING FOR OTHERS

Execution is an internal and external experience.

Internal for you and External for the person you are providing service for.

I recommend striving for an execution ratio of 2-to-1 (external to internal.)

Internal execution will be great for your confidence and standards.

Remember execution is for others and not yourself.

I try very hard to keep the other person or people in mind when I am executing for them.

Everyone that you interact with is important.

Do not become so concerned with the chain of authority.

The person you interact with may currently be at the bottom of the chain but that doesn't mean they will always be there.

I have increased my career opportunities by making conversations with receptionists and other representatives at prospective companies.

These receptionists and representatives have been my brand ambassadors.

People are paying attention to your actions.

GO THE EXTRA MILE

Going the extra mile is huge.

This can't be understated.

We hear it all the time.

What does this mean?

Do the absolute most you can for others.

In the concept is the word "extra".

Most people are not willing to do extra because they are focusing on what they can get instead of what they can give.

We fail to realize the power and the wonderful gift in giving and not receiving.

I know this may be a hard concept for most of us to understand.

I understand that you may currently be in a difficult situation and need receiving instead of giving.

You may be thinking "I will give when I am able to."

Most of the time this statement is not true.

When we are able, we still don't.

The reason for this is because of conditioning.

I always try to go the extra mile because I like to separate myself from others.

I want to be in a league of my own.

I have very high standards and require a lot from myself.

Delivering extra will reap great rewards.

I have received monetary and extrinsic rewards for going the extra mile.

The extra mile is like a strong punch from a boxer that knocks out their opponent

The opponent never sees it coming.

The people you are executing for won't either.

Exceptional people go the extra mile and are admired and celebrated.

COMMON ACTION: EXPERIENCE

We are not thoughtful about the experiences we create with others.

Most of us believe the experience is just another encounter that does not mean anything.

This is farther from the truth.

"If you are casual with your experiences, you will become a casualty."

"Why should I worry about creating intentional experiences this will not lead to anything?"

We become what we think about the most.

RECOMMENDED ACTION: EXPERIENCE

I recommend creating memorable experiences that enlighten others.

When I speak about enlightenment I am referring to attraction regarding vibration and frequency.

Electronic devices all have vibrations (energy) and frequencies (connections).

When a mobile phone attempts to connects to a Wi-Fi connection the frequencies will see if they are compatible.

The frequency will be as strong as the vibration.

The same is true for your career.

People like to associate with others they like, know, trust.

The greater the experience you can provide for someone the more they want to interact with you.

Providing a great experience to just one person can change your career forever.

PRINCIPLE 12: RESULTS

RESULTS INTRODUCTION

This is the most important principle in this book.

The previous 11 principles are great.

We are result based individuals.

Our careers will be determined by the results we produce.

Warning: Do not apply the previous 11 principles and forget to apply the most important one.

RESULTS ADJUSTOR

Results are connected to goals.

Goals provide focus and clarity for the results you want to achieve.

Life and career never goes according to plan.

You were promised a promotion or position and it was taken away.

You were informed that other colleagues' need to be evaluated before a final decision can be made.

You were close to the finish line.

Your progress will be delayed 6 months to a year.

You can be devastated.

You can be angry.

Your focus is your choice.

You can focus on how close you were to the goal.

You could also focus on the previous progress that was made.

You also have the opportunity to make the necessary adjustments.

I remember goals that I set over a decade ago.

I still have not achieve some of these goals.

I am closer now than I was a decade ago.

If I had given up anytime during the decade I would not be where I am now.

The only thing that is constant in life is change.

Most of us don't know how to embrace change.

This decision can lead to never achieving results.

A temporary delay is not a final denial.

I want to repeat that one more time to make sure that you understood the power in that sentence.

A temporary delay is not a final denial.

You were given a task to complete with a specific deadline.

At the last minute you were informed that the timetable has been pushed up.

You still need to "work your magic (execute)".

Make the necessary adjustments and get it done.

You are preparing to execute a project.

A prominent resource is no longer available.

The project will take longer to complete.

Once again make the necessary adjustments and get it done.

Most of the necessary adjustments are within our control.

Do not think about the decision too much.

Do or don't do.

DELIVER THE GOODS

Now is the time.

Deliver the goods you promised.

For example, you are working with a multi-million dollar company.

You promise the company that you can reduce their expenses by 30 percent in 3 months.

You need to deliver the goods.

The problem with most of us is that we don't deliver the goods.

We over promise on what we can provide to make a good impression.

However, we're making our brand look bad.

I believe that if you promise something you deliver on your promise.

Do not make promises that are hard to keep.

Do not inconvenience others because of your big mouth.

We make promises that are hard to keep because we want to talk a "big game".

We talk a "big game" because we compare ourselves to others.

You are unique.

You are your own person.

If you want the knowledge, confidence, and results others have then commit to creating new habits and disciplines.

You can achieve the same results.

Looking back on my career there have been several instances where I started small.

Now I have been entrusted with big responsibilities.

I started as a "delivery guy".

My only responsibility to mail legal documents to attorneys.

Years later I am a corporate trainer and results coach.

I would have never imagined this.

My responsibilities changed because I delivered the goods.

ALWAYS FINISH

Always finish what you start.

No matter how bad it is.

When I start a task, I strive to complete it even if it is difficult.

Plans will get off track.

Adjustments will be required.

People lose motivation to complete a goal.

Everything is not "wrapped in a perfect bow" for them to unwrap.

I don't agree with the "perfect bow" mentality.

If you can finish then finish.

The process of completing a goal may not be what you envisioned.

Achievement of the goal should be all that matters.

We make resources more important than resourcefulness.

Blaming a lack of resources is the primary reason why most goals go uncompleted.

Finishers are rewarded because they finish and produce results.

A sports team can win the game by one point.

A win is a win.

The sports team will focus more on the win than the tough game they just played.

They achieved their goal.

The goal was not achieved by their initial expectations but it was still accomplished.

They will take the win and celebrate accordingly.

TRUE CURRENCY

Results are the true currency.

Results are everything.

Talking about what you are going to do is useless.

Getting results is powerful.

Results can be validated.

Everyone knows the results.

We talk 10 times more than the results we produce.

Be a person that get results.

We are remembered for the results we produce.

Everyone you admire produces results you love.

This is the reason why you admire those people.

Do not get complacent.

In life and in your career, you will be evaluated by the results you produced lately.

CONSTANT DELIVERY

Deliver the results you are capable of.

Never be a "was" person.

Be a current person instead.

A "was" person is someone who produced great results in the past.

They no longer show they can deliver those same results.

I used to visit a casual restaurant frequently.

They served great food and delivered great service in the past.

This restaurant used to be one of my favorite places to eat.

Recently the food and service experience declined.

I stop going to the restaurant.

We all age.

I understand that in your youth you delivered the greatest results because of vitality.

Now that we are seasoned, we should not fade into the shadows.

I make an effort to remain a "hungry lion".

I do not get satisfied with my previous accomplishments.

One of my greatest fears is for my colleagues and superiors to refer to me in the past.

"He used to be great."

"He solved this problem."

"He solved that problem."

"We are not sure if he is still capable of such amazing results."

"If he is, we have not seen it recently."

My initial goal was to be great.

My current goal is to remain great.

I still participate in the basic departmental functions.

I want to show my departmental and divisional co-workers that I have not gotten lazy.

I don't rest on my laurels.

I like to show up to work every day.

I want to prove to everyone that "this lion" still likes to hunt.

We are only as good as our last delivery.

Make sure you deliver with excellence.

CALM AND RELAX

As mentioned previously things will not always go according to plan.

I recommend remaining calm and relaxed.

Stay focused and execute with excellence.

This is easier said than done.

I strongly believe that in order to remain calm and relaxed you need a strong mind.

To develop a strong mind, you need to feed it constantly (daily).

This is why Part I regarding mastery is so important.

Career Professionals that have achieved the highest level of mastery usually remain calm and relaxed when they are faced with difficult challenges.

They push though and execute.

Principle 9 regarding focus aids the foundational concepts of mastery.

Where ever your focus goes so does your execution.

I will explain 2 stories to you.

These stories will explain the importance of mastery and focus.

HUNGRY FOR A SUB

WEST PALM BEACH, FL – SUMMER- AFTERNOON

Stomachs are growling.

Time to eat.

I pull into the local supermarket.

Park the car.

I exit the car and head inside the supermarket.

I make my way to the deli.

I notice a long line.

My stomach continues to growl.

I am trying to stay focused on the sub instead of the long line of other customers in front of me.

Sammy the sandwich maker is ready for the next customer.

He signals for me to come forward.

I approach.

Sammy: What can I get for you today?

JS: I would like a sub. A whole sub with wheat bread.

Sammy: What type of cheese would you like?

JS: I will take white American.

Sammy: What type of sandwich would you like?

JS: Chicken tenders

Sammy proceeds to make my sub.

Sammy seems like he is having a rough day.

Our conversation continues and he becomes snarky with me.

I remain calm.

I know dealing with people is not an easy job.

In the past I had a job that required interaction with large quantities of people daily.

Based on my past experience I showed Sammy grace.

I decided not to focus on his attitude.

My goal was to get the sub I wanted.

I want to eat my sub when I got home.

The average person would have put Sammy in his place.

I did not think that was necessary.

Sammy's colleague Jason informed Sammy not to forget about a specific task.

This reminder angered Sammy.

Sammy started to lose focus.

He forgot one of my ingredients for the sub.

He remembered before it was too late and added it.

Jason was in Sammy's head.

Sammy continued to complete my sub.

He completed the sub incorrectly.

I did not correct him.

He was clearly upset.

I did not want to agitate him.

I decided I would just remove the extra ingredients later when I arrived home.

What is the lesson?

Sammy continued to focus on how mad Jason made him.

He also focused on finishing my sandwich quickly instead of accurately.

I was focused on remaining calm, being relaxed, and enjoying my sub.

I was able to do this because of mastering my mind.

Focus on what is really important and not the distractions.

TELLER ASSISTANCE

WEST PALM BEACH, FL – SUMMER- AFTERNOON

I needed to go to the bank to complete financial transactions.

I arrive in the parking lot.

I head inside the bank.

I wait in line.

I wanted to wait for my friend Karl to help me.

Stacy a new teller decided she wanted to assist me.

I granted her the opportunity.

She did not know she would be in for some challenges.

She learned valuable lessons.

Karl was there to help her if she got in trouble.

Stacy: How can I help you today?

JS: I have several transactions I need to complete.

Stacy: Ok

I gave her my license and bank card to look up my accounts.

She struggled initially.

She signaled Karl to assist.

Karl leaned over his station and guided Stacy through the screen navigation process.

Stacy was still new to banking.

She was only 3 months in.

Stacy was nervous.

Minutes later she found the account number

I had coins to deposit into my account.

Stacy counted the coins.

Most of the coins were wrapped in coin wrappers.

This made the process easier.

I helped her through her challenges.

I am a former banker.

I knew how to fix common mistakes.

I been there and made the same mistakes when I started in banking.

She learned a lot.

Stacy: Thank you for being patient. I made several mistakes today with your transactions.

JS: Today was a learning experience.

Remain positive.

Continue to work hard.

You will become more comfortable with the transactions with more practice and time.

Stacy took extended time to complete my transactions.

Her focus was on making sure that she completed them correctly.

I was pleased with her.

She kept her focus on the transactions.

Stacy and I had the same focus.

This is why my experience was more pleasurable at the bank with Stacy than at the supermarket deli with Sammy.

LAST MINUTE ESCALATIONS

A blessing and a curse.

I have achieved high levels of Mastery, Attraction, and Delivery (Execution).

What is the prize for this?

I receive important responsibilities known as last minute escalations (LME).

Most LME's can be resolved with appropriate planning and communication.

Unfortunately, 95% of the time this two crucial components are missing.

After completing so many LME's I welcome them.

When they arrive it is just another task that needs to be completed.

My departmental colleagues do not share my same sentiments.

They want everything to be perfect.

They want the normal time to complete a normal escalation.

The secret to completing LME's is muscle memory.

I have completed so many LME's with different scenarios that I am not afraid of the tight deadlines for delivery.

Remember "pressure make diamonds".

Become diamonds and shine bright.

HAVE FUN

When executing and producing excellent results we should have fun.

We're investing a lot of time, effort, and energy.

High-income earners and successful people are concerned about the results they produce.

They also try to have fun as well.

Having fun makes, the results enjoyable.

You have permission to smile.

You also have permission to thank yourself for working hard and producing results.

Engaging in activities we are passionate or highly interested in will lead to mastery.

Mastery in collaboration with execution can produce favorable results.

Lastly, always remain positive even on tough days.

There is a light at the end of the tunnel.

We must always believe that better and brighter days are ahead.

Having fun will lead to a more fulfilled career and more money in your bank account.

COMMON ACTION: RESULTS

A large percentage of us become overwhelmed when it comes to producing a specific result.

All of the previous hard work go down the drain.

We tend to deliver average results.

We are receiving our ideal level of compensation.

We want an increase in compensation then we will deliver the desired results.

Unfortunately, this is not how it works.

RECOMMENDED ACTION: RESULTS

I recommend delivering outstanding execution.

People will notice and will always want to do business with you.

We love winners and want to be associated with them.

Are you currently happy with your performance?

I have developed a practice to make decisions that I am proud of.

Every night I reflect on the day.

I evaluate my decisions and execution.

My goal is to be satisfied with my decisions.

I want to go to sleep every night in peace.

I want to know that I did the best that I could for the day.

Maybe this self-reflection exercise can assist you in making more satisfied decisions.

What if we fail to deliver outstanding execution?

Honestly self-evaluate yourself and make the necessary adjustments to improve your performance.

I assure you your confidence should remain in tack.

Be willing to give it another try until you get your desired results.

Deliver on your promises.

EPILOGUE

FINAL THOUGHTS

Thank you for taking the time to read this book.

I hope that I was able to provide value to you.

I hope this book inspired you take action on achieving your career goals as soon as possible.

Seek Mastery.

All high-income earners and successful people are masters at something.

You can join this elusive club.

Stop chasing money.

Decide to master your passionate career choice.

The foundational principles of *MASTERY*:

Knowledge

Continual learning

Practice and

Adaptability.

Next, become great at attracting the necessary business partners you will need to achieve your career goals.

ATTRACTION can be obtained through building an

Excellent brand

Effective marketing

Great networking and

Persuasive and influential advertising.

Finally, deliver the goods and be exceptional at delivering great results.

Exceptional ***execution*** can be obtained by

Laser focus

Strong collaborative teamwork

Creating memorable experiences and

Consistently delivering amazing results.

My wish for you is to implement these 12 principles as soon as you can.

Go achieve your career goals in half the time and half the stress.

Best wishes in your career endeavors, have fun and enjoy the process!

ABOUT THE AUTHOR

Joe A Simmons is a 14-year business veteran specializing in Peak Performance Training and Coaching. Joe has been privileged to utilize his knowledge and experience at 3 Billion Dollar Corporations resulting in hundreds of millions of dollars in sales. In addition to the sales results, Joe has also reduced expenses for the Billion Dollar Corporations resulting in millions of dollars as well. Joe has trained over 200 colleagues throughout his career. Joe currently lives in Palm Beach County, Florida with his family.

www.ingramcontent.com/pod-product-compliance
Lightning Source LLC
Chambersburg PA
CBHW060038210326
41520CB00009B/1181